I0697674

DEDICATION

I dedicate this book to my family. My family will always be my priceless treasure.

TABLE OF CONTENTS

The Sail of Marriage

How to Save the Sinking Marriage

By: Juliet Williams

9781635010503

PUBLISHERS NOTES

Disclaimer – Speedy Publishing LLC

This publication is intended to provide helpful and informative material. It is not intended to diagnose, treat, cure, or prevent any health problem or condition, nor is intended to replace the advice of a physician. No action should be taken solely on the contents of this book. Always consult your physician or qualified health-care professional on any matters regarding your health and before adopting any suggestions in this book or drawing inferences from it.

The author and publisher specifically disclaim all responsibility for any liability, loss or risk, personal or otherwise, which is incurred as a consequence, directly or indirectly, from the use or application of any contents of this book.

Any and all product names referenced within this book are the trademarks of their respective owners. None of these owners have sponsored, authorized, endorsed, or approved this book.

Always read all information provided by the manufacturers' product labels before using their products. The author and publisher are not responsible for claims made by manufacturers.

This book was originally printed before 2014. This is an adapted reprint by Speedy Publishing LLC with newly updated content designed to help readers with much more accurate and timely information and data.

Speedy Publishing LLC

40 E Main Street, Newark, Delaware, 19711

Contact Us: 1-888-248-4521

Website: http://www.speedypublishing.co

REPRINTED Paperback Edition: ISBN: 9781635010503

Manufactured in the United States of America

CHAPTER 1- BEFORE TYING THE KNOT AND GETTING MARRIED

Marriage is the most delicate and in most of the cases most important relationship known in this world. Our life has become very rigid and busy and this rigid life has made lots of things go wrong and one of the very important areas is marriage which gets affected due to our unhealthy, unsocial and sometimes senseless living style.

There are certain things that you need to know and need to implement in your life and without these things you will be deprived of all those happy moments of your life. According to a research ratio of divorce and separation has increased with time and there are endless reasons for this increased ratio.

In this book I will guide you towards making your marriage a healthier and happy relationship. You need to know that mending your marriage is very important to live a healthy and prosperous life because I have seen people who screw up their marriage but they not only screw their marriage instead when marriage is screwed then, everything in your life is screwed because it effects on almost every field of your life.

When your marriage runs smoothly then, you feel very relaxed and there is almost zero stress in your life. This less stress increases your productivity and allows you to concentrate more on your work instead of always thinking about your relationship.

I have gathered information from lots of sources and then tried to align everything up so that you can have a better understanding of everything.

If you are thinking about getting into relationship of marriage or you are already running a marriage or even if you have some troubles in your marriage then, you should keep reading this book and you will get answers of almost every question that comes in your mind.

There are two kinds of lives that every one of us lives and these two lives are life as single and life as married person. There are lots of differences in both of these lives that everyone needs to understand and if you cannot understand those differences and take both of these lives as same then, things will start to get fussy. Especially when you do not change and do not adapt to married conditions and you keep sticking up with those old single routine then, things can get very difficult for your marriage. There are certain things that you need to know before indulging into your married life and following discussion will reveal those things.

Select Your Partner Carefully

First and most important thing is to search and select for the right person who can accompany you for the rest of your life. This can be crucial as hell but sometimes it becomes very easy job to do. In both of the cases you should never hurry into a relationship and spend some time together before marriage.

This will allow you to know that how much different your personalities are and how many adjustments you will have to make to survive into that relationship. If you can identify that you two are synchronizing with each other well and there are not many differences arising during your relationship then, you can trust your senses and move towards a healthier and more stronger married relationship but if you are finding it difficult to solve that person's attitude and you have a thinking that everything will be fine after marriage then, believe me nothing is going to be right after marriage because things can only get worse after marriage.

Know Yourself and Know The Other Person

This is an important aspect which helps you in choosing the right person. First of all, you should know yourself properly and know your limitations, attitude attributes and similar other things and then try to look for similar sort of person. Knowing yourself means that you should be always show yourself as you are to the other person. It is often seen that people often lie or make things up while looking to build a relationship but this is not the right way to do it. Similarly know the other person well by asking simple things about beliefs and other similar things. These simple questions will lead you to a more detailed understanding of that person's attitude and possible problems with his or her attitude.

Living, Loving and Sharing Should Be There

If you are starting a new relationship then, it is necessary that you give him or her proper time to understand you and this time should not only include meeting and doing dinner together but there are so many other things that you need to show to the other person. If love and care are absent in those early days then, you can never expect these things with the course of life. These are very basic needs of relationship and their absence means that the other person is either not ready to make a relationship or he or she is not well-composed for being with you.

Try To Listen More Than Saying

Listening is also another very important aspect of relationships and especially when you are in early stage of your relationships then, it is necessary that you should listen to the other person to know his or her views about different aspects of life. It is often seen that people tend to talk more than listen but you should be equal in both of these things and after making yourself clear once, listen to the other person carefully and try to know that what he or she is trying to tell you from their views and talks.

Be Ready To Make Some Adjustments and Face Some Troubles

This is an understood thing that whenever you are looking to build a new relationship then, it will go through some troubles and problems but if you started to panic in these problems then, things will get worse. These small troubles and differences will lead you to know that how much accepting the other person is. If he or she is totally rattled with these problems then, you should think about some alternate option and look for a better person but you need to keep yourself composed in these conditions and try to make sure that the other person is not getting an expression that you are willing to make any sacrifice for that relationship instead make some small adjustments if needed and make her believe that you are trying to make everything work.

Strengthening Your Relationship

In the above chapter you have learned all the important things that are necessary to understand before making any relationship but now we will move another step further and I will tell you some important that will tell you after making a relationship. Making a commitment or relationship is easy but it is very hard to make that relationship work. If you are not aware of some basic ingredients to work that relationship then, you will end up breaking up that relationship or either getting yourself lost in the complexities of those relations. It is especially helpful in husband wife relationship that you have to take care for each other well and try to make your relationship work in a healthier manner.

Mutual Responsibility

Responsibility is the key in husband wife relationship but some people often misunderstand this responsibility clause and think that husband is the only one responsible for everything in this relationship. This is not the case because both partners are equaled responsible in making the relationship work. If any one of them thinks that he or she is not responsible then things will start to get bad. The types of responsibilities are different for both of the partners. Wife's role is more of a supportive one while husband has to handle everything with care. Small misunderstandings will always arise but if you are responsible enough to accept your fault then, these misunderstanding will make your relationship even stronger.

Include Care in Your Relationship

This is human nature that we always love to get care. This is true in husband wife relationship because the more you care for each other, stronger will become your relationship. Care is also a mutual action because if you are not caring for the other partner then, he or she will also not bother to care about you.

Care is not something very hard and precise thing that you cannot do instead there are some very small things included in this care. For example if you can just give an extra phone call to your wife for asking her that how she is feeling and for telling her that you always remember her, will make it a huge gesture for your wife.

Similarly if you are a wife then, just a soothing smile to your husband, when he comes home after a tiring day in office, is enough to make him believe that you always care for him. You can consider it just as an emotional bank account and you have to deposit all the good feeling, better gestures and caring words in that bank account. If you do not deposit enough of this stuff in that emotional bank account then, you cannot expect anything in return.

Get Rid Of Communication Gap

Communication gap is another very important factor that can make your relationship weaker. In new relationships communication is the key and without proper communication you will not be able to tell your partner that how much you care for him or her neither you will be able to tell them that what kind of attitude you have. If you tell less then ultimately you will also know less. To know the other person well, you must speak a lot and try to know everything that you can. It is not necessary that you should ask only about some very crucial and big issues but you can start from very normal and easy going discussions and then progress onto some more complex issues of life.

Too much speaking and very less listening is also not very healthy for relationships because in that way you will not be able to know the other person very well. The best way to communicate and know the other person is to clear yourself completely and then listen to the other person carefully. This increased communication will not only help you in making the relationship stronger but it also helps you in decreasing the misunderstandings more effectively because whenever something goes wrong with your relationship then, you can talk our everything and matter can be solved carefully.

Proper Time for Your Relationship

Timing is also crucial and you need to make sure that you are giving enough time to your relationship. In fact less time allocation to relationship is the major reason of break ups these days. Life is very busy these days and most of the people work day in and day out to survive and to meet their living standards in this society but in this struggle of making money, relationships are often overlooked and people suffer from break ups.

If you are a husband or an earning wife then, you should analyze your weekly schedule and try to determine that how much time you are giving to your family and your partner. This analysis will tell you that how much you need to work on your relationship and how much more time you need to give to your relationship timing also includes that you should break that old routine and habit of 9-5 some times. Bring an element of surprise in your relationship and come home from your office early sometimes. This small gesture will cost you nothing but will make your partner very happy and he or she will think that you care for them.

Trust

Trust is another very important thing and you can say that it is also one of the mutual feelings that you need to develop between your relationships. If you do not trust your partner then, you cannot expect your partner to trust you. Trust does also not just about believe that your partner will not cheap upon you but it also means that you should know that your partner can never go against his or her responsibilities related to that relationship.

All of the above mentioned things are very easy to implement in your daily life and they do not include anything that is very complex and if you do little extra try then, these things can make your relationships very strong and healthy. Good relationships and tension free relationships can also make your physical life better because tension is always harmful for health.

Chapter 2- The Possibility of a Controlled and Strengthened Marriage

Misunderstandings and miscommunications are very common things in today's marriages and most of these things come due to mishandling of this relationship. You must know that husband wife relationship is very delicate relationship that needs lots of care and attention from both parties to stay on the path. Following discussion will tell you that what are those basic needs that you need to fulfill for a comprehensive and stronger marriage.

Make Some Rules and Follow Them

Living less than one roof can be tough at times and especially when you come from different back grounds then, it becomes even tougher to cope with all those differences that you have integrated in each other's personalities. There is simple method that can help you in living without any troubles. You need to make some rules in the house and then make sure that you both follow those rules.

The Sail of Marriage

It is often seen that husband and wives do not tend to tell each other their likes and dislikes but things can be lot easier and simpler if you can just say your opinion in open. For example instead of sitting quiet in the back seat and biting your nails, you can just tell your partner that he should drive under or less than specific speed because just assuming that he will know what you want will not make that happen. Similarly there can be so many other simple rules that you can make and these rules, if followed properly can save you from lots of misunderstandings.

Helping Each Other

When you live under one roof then, there are certain responsibilities that you both need to fulfill. If you are husband then, you are bound to help your safe in daily households and especially on weekends you need to make sure that you are with your wife in almost everything because she also needs rest and you're very little help will give a very great feeling to her.

Similarly if you are a wife then, it is your responsibility that you should make your husband as comfortable as you can. If you greet your husband home with a cute smile then, it will make everything better and your husband will get a feeling that his whole day's work is well spent but if you start yelling at your husband right after his entrance in the house then, it will start to increase the tension and your husband will not be very comfortable with that.

Never Let the Romance Die From Your Relationship

When you have spent some time with your partner then, most of the times it happens that your relationship become predictable and everything becomes known. Even people add romance in that predictable nature but this is not the right approach to adopt instead you should try and keep romance alive throughout your relationship. Romance is not just about having sex in the bed but there are so many thing that can make your relationship more romantic.

If you are coming from the office and you see a flower shop on the way then, bringing a simple flower bucket is also included in romance and this small and almost inexpensive gesture can make your life very romantic and can create a very pleasant feeling about you in the heart of your partner. So keep doing similar gestures to keep romance alive in your relationship.

Financial Stability

Financial stability is another thing that leads to a long lasting relationship because financial stability gives you very stable place in society and decreases lots of your stress and daily tensions. Some people complain that their wives do not give them support in bad financial situations but this is not the case unless you are too lazy to change your financial status.

If you are sincere with the cause and trying your best to do better in life then, there is no girl in this world who will not stand with you in hard times but problems start when you stop trying for the best. Always give you best shot and then, you can expect support for your partner. Similar is the case with wife that of she sees that her husband is unable to fulfill all the financial requirements of the family then, she should work and support her husband in every way that she could.

As a married couple, it is a different life altogether that you have to live. There are lots of compromises that you have to make and at the same time, there are lots of things that you always have to do against your will but all of this is for the bigger benefits of your future. If you can make some slight compromises to make your coming life easier and healthier then, there is nothing wrong in that and you should never insert your ego in these matters. In the above discussions, I have told you that how you can select your perfect partner and then I told you that what are the things that can make your marriage more effective and longer lasting? In this discussion I am going to tell you about some things and strategies that you can adopt in case of any misunderstanding or any confusion that has happened in your relationship.

Always Think Positive and Accept The Responsibility

This is an understood thing that whenever a misunderstanding occurs then, it is not from one side only and both partners hold equal shares in that fight. This is a fact that very few people can accept because everyone starts to play the blame game and no one accepts his or her faults. This attitude should be corrected and you need to be brave enough that you should say ok I did or said this wrong and I am sorry for that. Once you have said and realized that fault or mistake was on your end then, it becomes easier for the other person to accept his or her fault too. You need to be positive about your relationship and never think about breaking up the relationship instead always look for a way out.

Unconditional Happiness

Some people associate happiness with certain things like if they will go on vacation then, they will be happier but living in home is dull and boring for them. This should be not the case because life is full of happiness and you need to just search smaller but very enjoyable moments of life in everyday life. For example when you play basketball with your kid then, it also should bring some happiness. Similarly when your daughter helps you out first time in the kitchen then, it should also bring happiness for you and similar other smaller things. These days' people often forget about these smaller happy moments and they are always looking for some big occasions and this attitude is also not very helpful for relationship and creates stress and tension.

If You Want Your Partner to Change Then Change Yourself First

Some people always want to integrate some unique things in their lives and these unique things become very difficult to integrate in the lives of other person. This is not the right way to change someone instead you need to initiate change from yourself and bring some changes that your partner likes. When you will bring those changes in your personality then, your partner will be automatically motivated to change him or herself because he or she will know that you have respected their ideas and changed yourself so now it becomes their responsibility to bring the changes that you like.

Forgiveness Can Make Your Relationship More Concrete And Invincible

As I have mentioned above that life has become very tough these days and there is not much time to look after each other. This busy life has also taken forgiveness and tolerance away from this society and wherever you see, there is a situation like chaos and extreme stress. No one is ready to forgive even the smallest of mistake of others. If you also have that kind of unforgiving attitude then, you need to change it for greater cause and to make your relationship more concrete. Forgiveness always helps to build relationships and when you forgive small mistakes of your partner then, he or she starts to respect you more and smaller misunderstandings can never shatter your relationship.

Spirituality Can Bring Harmony and Modesty in Your Relationship

Our life has become too much materialistic and there is very little margin of spirituality available. To exercise spirituality, it is not necessary for you to have faith in a certain religion but you just need to be very straight about your opinions and try to make your life smoother by practicing some mind cooling exercises. These exercises can help you a lot in bringing about the calmness and modesty in your approach towards relationship.

CHAPTER 3- GETTING TO KNOW MORE TO PREVENT BREAK UP

Disagreements are part of relationships but these disagreements should never shatter your relationships and you should find a way out. Even some disagreements can make your relationship stronger in a sense that they give you a chance to know each other better. Following are some tips that you need to follow and you can avoid all types of disagreements and break ups.

Know the Family Differences

There can be lots of problems in your new relationships but to solve that problem you need to understand the family differences. There can be lots of different patterns and traditions in both of your families and to adopt these traditions and family patterns you will need to do some compromises. This is also a mutual understanding that you have to adopt and both the partners are needed to participate in this setting actively.

Give Proper Time to Your Relationship

Timing is also crucial in every relationship and especially when you are in a new relationship then, it is necessary to give proper time to your relationship. Life can be very busy and especially these days you have to work very hard to meet your daily needs but relationships always need care and time. You also need to break that routine that develops with time. Always have an element of surprise in your daily life. Even if you have met some fight or misunderstanding then, you should give each other some time to settle in. if you start to make efforts to resolve everything right after the fight then, it could make things worse.

Emotional Support Is Important

Emotional support means that you need to accept the differences that you have in each other's lives. There is a saying that you need to agree to disagree. This saying is very true and very concrete that you have to execute in your daily relationship. You also need to give some support to your partner and realize about his or her position carefully. You need to understand that adjustments should be made from both ends. You should play your role while allow the other partner to play his or her role.

Agree To Disagree Is the Best Policy

Here can be two situations in your life, whether you can have a fight or break up and you will never want a patch up but there can be a different situation in which you can be itching to patch up. In that situation you should agree to disagree and accept your faults. This can be the simplest solution of your problems and is also very effective. I have seen people that become victim of their egos and they never accept that there is anything wrong with them instead they keep playing the blame game that makes things worse for them. Avoid that attitude and develop an accepting and responsible attitude to save your relationships.

Clarify Things and Then Listen To The Other Person

This is another very commonly found problem that when some misunderstanding happens between the couple then, both of the partners do not listen to each other and they keep telling their point of views separately. This is not the right approach and it will never solve your problems instead you need to adopt an approach of doing everything clear once and then start to listen to the other partner. This will allow you to clear your front and also listen to the other person and it can make things lit better and easier to understand. In short, you can say that you should be a very good listener and apply those listening skills in your relationship.

Always Be On the Point In Your Misunderstandings

This is another very common mistake that most of the couples make that they start the blame game and once some misunderstanding is developed then, they keep bringing everything from past in that misunderstanding. This should be avoided because it makes things complex and you should be always on point about a certain misunderstanding. Do not stray from the core issue and try to resolve it as one issue rather than mixing all the past issues in it and confusing each other about the solution.

General Tips

If you are married and looking for advice then, the above mentioned tips and methods can really help you in saving your marriage and you can make your marriage a very strong bond between two souls. There are some other important things also there that can really help you in being true soul mates. Following are those remaining things that can help you to make your relationship more concrete and healthy.

Knowing Each Other Truly

I have mentioned this point above also that knowing each other is very important and especially when you have to live the rest of the life together then, it becomes very important that you should know all the views and thoughts of each other about all the different things and scenarios. In that process of knowing each other you should be well-prepared to face the confrontations and disagreements but at the same time yo9u need to be very humble as you will be challenged about your views and will be given some different choices to adopt. You should analyze those choices positively and think about all aspects. If some suggestions are feasible then, accept them with an open heart.

Do Not Be Too Desperate

These days most of the people come from broken families and this situation makes them very desperate at times that they make wrong choices in search of a family. This is true that you should always look for a better life but in that struggle you should not forget that there is your own life also at stack and a wrong choice about your partner or similar other choice can ruin your whole life. Take your time and make choice after some research and as mentioned above after knowing each other well.

Understand Other Person's Perspective

It is very hard at times to understand other person's perspective about different things but this is very crucial too because without reaching at the exact level of other person, you will not be able to communicate and tell him or her exactly how you feel. In order to make sure that you have understood everything and whole personality of other person you need to see things from his eyes and try to think in the way he or she thinks. This will allow you to convey your own idea more clearly too because when you will start understanding him then, you will be able to adopt those ways which are more convenient and closer to his approach and his thoughts.

Take Responsibility of Your Words And Actions Thoroughly

I have described this fact throughout this book and it is very important too that you need to be responsible for your own actions words and similar other gestures. You need to stop blaming each other for faults and misunderstanding and prepare yourself to take half of the action on you. This will make the relation easier and you will be able to solve many problems very easily. Especially when both of the persons are willing to accept their differences then, it really becomes a smooth ride altogether.

Grow Together With Time

This is also very crucial part of any relationship that people always expect the other person to remain same even after 5 or 10 years have passed but this should be not the approach because time changes lots of things and similar is the case with personalities. You need to accept those changes and in fact you need to welcome those changes that come with time. If you start resisting to those changes then, things will get tough for the other person and he or she will also resist to your changes. So to protect and flourish your relationships never accept your partner to remain same throughout the life.

Believe And Trust Are the Keys To Successful Marriage

Believe and trusts are two of the mile stones for building a successful marital relationship. If these two things are present then, your life can be a bed of roses while their absence can make your life harder than you imagined. Both of these feelings are mutual and when one partner starts to trust the other then, other will also respect and trust you. This is human nature that if wife checks the cell phone and call record of husband then, husband will also spy on his wife. To avoid such situations, you should keep trust and believe as the catalyst for your relationship.

Chapter 4- Marriage's Up and Down

One of the main reasons for problems arising within the marriage relationship is the element of incompatibility. Once the initial excitement of the new relationship wears out, the couple soon finds themselves locked in a situation where they share nothing in common. This can be something positive if handled well, but it usually ends up bringing a lot of negativity into the equation and this eventually leads to the breakup of the marriage.

In order to be able to ensure the relationship has a better chance of survival; both parties should question their roles and perceptions linked to the relationship. You should discuss compatibility, understanding, cooperation, similar hobbies, types of interests, points of disagreements and joy and any other elements that would dictate the kind of participation either party will extend towards the relationship. When it comes to the negative aspect within the relationship, both parties should be acutely aware of how these situations are tackled and the duration the negativity is present until there is some resolution in sight. There will also be a need to examine how these resolutions are sought and incorporated for the aim of getting the relationship back on track.

These questions are well worth exploring within the beginnings of the relationship as this is helpful in dictating the eventual course the relationship will take. It is also be a good way to gauge the potential for pursuing this particular relationship and what the eventual goals expected are.

Enjoy Your Date

In order for a relationship to work, both parties must be equally committed to the idea of making the relationship work as best as possible. This includes exploring ways to spend time with each other without the need to be forced into doing so.

Making an effort to spend time together is very important if the couple intends to grow the relationship and to keep it happy and healthy for a long time to come. Without the effort to spend quality time together, the couple may find themselves eventually drifting apart and this may even lead to the eventual possibility of divorce. It is especially important to make time for each other, especially if both parties live very active and hectic professional lives. When this happens, it becomes very easy to use work and other distractions as an excuse to not make time for each other. This or course is a very bad habit to have surface during a relationship.

The following are some recommendations on how to create the ideal platform for spending quality time together to keep the relationship current and strong:

• Before the relationship actually gets to the present stage, both parties will have done things together that were enjoyable enough for them to consider taking the next step in establishing a relationship. Therefore, making the effort to continue to indulge in these same activities will be beneficial to the relationship.

• Finding new things to do together that both parties will enjoy is another good way to create the opportunity to spend some time together as a couple. These new activities should ideally be the kind that both parties will enjoy, however sometimes it may be necessary to indulge in something that only one of the partners really enjoy.

Keeping up the Spice

When it comes to keeping any relationship alive and exciting, there is usually the need to spice up things occasionally. This can be done through the use of love letters or perhaps going on date nights.

In the initial stages of the new relationship, these two activities are very much indulged in and even expected. However, sadly, as the relationship progresses to a more familiar phase, both parties may start taking each other for granted and one of the most popular ways of the perception becoming evident within the relationship is the lack of love letters and date nights. Most people make the mistake of thinking that such indulgences are no longer needed or necessary, thus falling into the rather boring routine that will eventually lead to the relationship getting into troubled waters.

Couples who fail to continue these activates as the relationship progresses, risk being taken for granted, and when outside opportunities present themselves, there is always the possibility of being tempted to indulge in these temptations as they will find ways to justify such indulgences.

The Sail of Marriage

Therefore, in the quest to not only keep the relationship as exciting as first perceived, the couple should continue the exchange of love letters and date nights to also ensure there are no temptations to seek such activities elsewhere. Being active in the activities will also allow the couple to look forward to these endearing times and also ensure both parties are constantly committed to putting their "best foot forward" at all times. This would include both the physical and mental aspects within the relationship.

Chapter 5- Keep the Dating Stages During Marriage

During the dating stages, everyone usually goes the extra mile to appear appealing and at their best. However sadly, this is not so when the couple become comfortable with each other and are already in the relationship for some time. Experts on the subject strongly suggest not letting one's physical appearance be neglected. This is also true when it comes to the mental growth of the individual in a committed relationship.

People don't seem to understand the importance of keeping up on both these fronts. Neither party will be interested in coming home to a relationship where there is no effort put into keeping each other excited and guessing. Boredom will usually be the result of such disinterest and this will eventually force both parties to seek excitement outside the existing relationship. There is always the danger of the stay at home partner being the one that eventually allows the mental and physical appearance to go downhill. Some people just don't seem to understand the impact made on each other when there is a total lack of interest in the general upkeep, both mentally and physically. This is especially so when there are so many temptations outside the marriage perimeter, this often reminds the straying party of exactly what they are missing out on. This is often also one of the main reasons why there is infidelity and discord within a relationship that has been in existence for quite some time.

Busy schedules and commitments are often the excuses given for the lack of focus on keeping oneself in the best of conditions, both mentally and physically. If both parties don't make a concerted effort to look good for each other, it certainly gives the impression of not valuing the relationship enough.

Love in the Air

Making a spouse feel important and loved in a relationship will definitely benefit both parties as the effort made will not go unnoticed for long. Making someone feel important is not only a delightful way of expressing love and respect for the person, but is also another way of cherishing the loved one.

Happily married couples will almost always attest to the fact that treating each other with respect and love goes a long way in keeping the relationship strong and being able to stand the test of time. Besides the more obvious reason such as love and respect for the spouse, this treatment will also show the level of value the individual puts on the existence of the spouse within the context of the relationship. It will also be a very natural corresponding action to return from the receiving party, thus making the relationship even stronger and longer lasting.

The more popular way of extending the attitude of putting the spouse foremost in thought and deed would be to always consult the spouse when important decision are to be made that would affect each other. Others may include finding ways to keep the spouse happy and contented within the relationship, by making a conscious effort to indulge in or arrange for activities that would make the spouse feel special and loved and even buying small gifts for no particular reason, except to express love. Simple acts that don't cause a lot of work or money such as opening a door or pulling out a chair for the spouse will go a long way in making the spouse feel special and loved. Always choosing to spend quality time with the spouse whenever the opportunity presents itself is also one way of putting the spouse on the top of the list.

The Importance Of Saving A Marriage

Marriage is not something that should be taken lightly and this is even more so when there are signs within the relationship that signify some level of trouble brewing. Most people try to take the necessary steps to save the marriage before throwing in the towel or raising the white flag in defeat.

Every marriage is worth saving, and it would certainly be worth the effort to try and salvage what was once something beautiful and wonderful. This is even more important of an exercise if there are children involved. The following are some ways to explore if both parties are really interested in making an attempt to save the marriage:

• Set aside some time to talk about things that have caused the marriage to lose its luster. This may not be easy to do without outside help such as a support group or counseling sessions. Attempting to do so without guidance may cause the couple to get into an argument or worse, into a fighting match where unfounded accusations will make the situation even worse.

• Genuinely seeking another chance to make the marriage work is another option to explore in the quest towards saving the marriage. Sometimes asking for another chance and then taking all the necessary steps to ensure genuine effort is made will help both parties view the marriage in a different light. Active participation towards the end goal of saving the marriage will require commitment and perseverance.

• Some people may decide to make physical life changing decisions in order to prove their sincerity toward wanting to save the marriage. These may include changing jobs, relocating to a quieter neighborhood to create a better quality of life or even new activities.

There really is not a point in giving up on a marriage and wasting many years and much effort. As long as there is still love in the picture there is still a chance of fixing things. However, it is important to know when a relationship is better ended such as toxic or abusive situations. If there is still a spark there though you should definitely try some of the above tips to fix your marriage, after all some people believe you only get one shot at true love.

Chapter 6- Take Marriage Counseling

It is often difficult to try and save the marriage when both parties feel they are hitting a brick wall with their perceived attempts to being reasonable.

The marriage counselor is usually an individual who is not interested in taking side but more interested in getting to the root of the problem and finding a workable solution to get the marriage back on the right track. These people are usually specifically trained to help any and all situations that are created within the marriage that has gone badly wrong. Couple seeking the help of a marriage counselor, will usually come away quite surprised, at what they learn from the sessions.

In almost all cases, miscommunication and misinterpretation are the main culprits of the discord experienced within the marriage.

The Sail of Marriage

The marriage counselor will be able to help the couple see things in a different light and then outline ways to help create a more conducive and workable situation where both parties can participate positively towards mending the relationship.

In helping the couple identify the problem both honestly and clearly, the counselor will then be able to get both parties to work on some exercises that will help them to understand each other better, thus allowing the couple to better face the problem head on when the appropriate time presents itself.

Attending marriage counseling session would also help the couple be more open as the counselor will certainly ask very probing question and will not allow either party to be evasive in their answers.

This level of honestly is sometimes not forthcoming within the confines of the marriage.

Make a List of Goals for Your Marriage

Although it may seem ideal to simply drift along through the marriage, it would help to create a stronger marriage bond if both parties work out some goals they can participate in achieving.

The goal setting exercise is important as it helps both parties strengthen their relationship by focusing on a common goal. It also helps to improve communication and creates the desire to help each other in a more conducive manner so that the goals set can be achieved without undue pressure.

The goals also help to validate each other's contributions to the relationship and also keep both parties accountable and committed.

Part of the goal setting process would require both parties to verbalize their dreams and aspirations for the relationship, thus giving each other a clear insight into the workings of their individual mindsets.

Creating a list individually and then taking the time to sit down together to try and collaborate in forming a new list that will serve each party's needs comfortably, would be the ideal way to go about the whole exercise of setting goals.

Once this is done, both parties would then have to decide on some sort of time line that would be suitable and realistic in moving towards achieving the goals set.

This would include having to evaluate and revaluate certain values and mindset in order to make the goals set achievable. This time of sharing aspirations can be very enjoyable and enlightening if both parties maintain some level of intimacy and cordiality. Being accusational and demanding will not help the exercise of goal setting for the marriage. The act of sharing goals can often bring a couple closer together and also keep them more focused on each other throughout the exercise.

Once the goals for the marriage has been firmly outlined and accepted, there would be some follow up steps that should be taken to ensure the goals set are achieved without eventually contributing to the downfall of the relationship.

Making a list of the elements that could be possible contributing factors in not getting the goals achieved would be a wise and preemptive action to initiate. This will give both parties the leeway to be open and frank about their reservations and fears. It will also allow both parties to see each other weakness and strengths and work toward exploring the strengths and limiting the hold that the weaknesses may present.

There are several things that would constitute actions that get in the way of achieving the end goals for the marriage. Some of these may prove to be unfounded and quite easily managed and eradicated, while others may present more of a challenge to the couple. The ones that would be identifies as a challenge should be addressed without reservations to ensure these challenges don't test the patience of both parties and also to ensure it does not in any way negatively affect the marriage.

Sometimes there is a need to prioritize the items on the list of marriage goals. Failing to do this could create the confusion and stress that could lead to the goals becoming a nightmare rather than a healthy focus for the couple. Being prepared and aware of the necessity to change priorities would also be another thing to consider and work on, as more often than not situations arise unexpectedly that can cause the goals set to become defunct. Part of the list should be how to handle or address such possibilities.

CHAPTER 7- POSITIVE AFFIRMATION AND POSITIVE ATTITUDE ARE NEEDED

Part of the growing process within a marriage relationship is to understand and accept the need for positive intervention when things are not going according to plan. Being able to seek such help is pivotal in keeping the marriage of the road to recovery rather than disaster.

The most difficult effort to make would be to not resort to seeking justice for the wronged feelings and experiences. The individual would have to be strong enough and to want the relationship badly enough, to get to the stage where there is a positive attitude in place to help salvage the marriage by getting help.

Bitterness will not help in any way, especially if the individual is interested in keeping a good grasp on the relationship. Despite the hurt and negativity, both parties should ideally try to seek help from professional outside forces that will help to move both parties forward and in a mode where damage control can be initiated.

Trusting that the help sought, will give both parties the opportunity to seek some form of resolve that will help to keep the marriage on the track to mending itself is very important.

In most cases the trust issue within relationship is the first thing that becomes a matter of contention for both parties, therefore making the effort to develop a positive attitude to building back the trust is an important step in the right direction.

Forgiveness is another element that needs to be addressed in the process of cultivating a positive attitude. The positive impact of being ready to forgive can and usually does wonders for the failing relationship.

A lot of people have attested to the success of salvaging the marriage when the positive element of forgiveness is widely and consciously practiced.

It's You

Most relationships that encounter problems seem to focus on the "who is to blame" element. This is not only destructive but is also an action that usually leads to more problems than solutions.

Being the "bigger" person within the equation, would allow the individual to take on the responsibility of acknowledging some change is needed, and that the change should ideally start with the individual itself.

Being prepared to accept that some of the fault does indeed lie at the individual's "feet" is a set in the right direction. Taking the time and effort to explore the various reasons and actions that had a part in contributing to the current negativity of the relationship will help the individual realize that there is really no benefit in placing the blame on everyone and anyone else.

Successful recovery of a damaged relationship will be off to a good start when each person involved is willing to change for the better.

This should be the main focus of the exercise as changing for the better will always be a more beneficial exercise that will eventually become so normal that the individual will no longer look upon such an exercise as something forced or unfair.

The positive changes will also help the individual become a better person, thus making the overall situation more pleasant and easy to improve upon.

It is also almost always easier to change oneself rather than trying to change the other party in the relationship. Changing oneself does not require the constant maneuvering of another person's physical and mental control.

Concentrating on being a better person and a more loving and caring partner will also encourage the other party to respond in an equally positive manner thus successfully allowing the relationship to improve for the better.

Look for Free Counseling

Marriage is hard work and anyone who says otherwise is not really committed to making it for the long haul. Along with the hard work there are also times of great joy and fulfillment, but when this is not forthcoming for quite a while, then, it is time to seek some outside help. This help ideally should come in the form of marriage counseling.

The following are some places that one should explore for the purpose of seeking outside help to try and save or create a better and stronger marriage relationship:

Reading as much as possible on the subject would be helpful. When there are problems published that are similar to the ones the individual is going through the general experience and outcome could be applied or at least tried. Sometimes it would be helpful to know that there are others that have gone through the same situation and that it is possible to overcome it successfully.

Seeking counseling from a priest is also another option for those who are more religiously inclined. This is helpful only if both parties are open and willing to explore options that are closely linked to the religious angle or take on things.

This is also a very helpful option, if both parties are known to the priest taking on the counseling session, as it would give all concerned a better and clearly take on the whole situation.

For some joining a support group would be a more suitable match, as they would prefer to hear several different views on the matter and also for its non threatening and non judgmental base.

Being in a group will allow both parties to be able to hear several different types or suggestions and opinions that may prove to be helpful and practical.

Sometimes when a marriage seems to be in trouble, both parties will ignore the sign in the hope that things will eventually work themselves out and everything will be ok in the end. However in most cases this is never the ideal outcome and things just escalate further until it becomes so unbearable that the only solution would be divorce. Therefore in the interest of trying to save a marriage, all efforts should be exercised to keep the idea of divorce from creeping into the situation.

The following are some of the more obvious signs that could indicate that a marriage is in trouble and what action should be taken to avoid disastrous consequences:

One of the first signs of trouble in "paradise" is when one party can no longer see the good in the other person. Anything and everything said or done by the other party is almost always looked upon with disdain, disappointment or even worse anger.

This is a sure sign that things are not right and is help is not sought immediately; a once loving relationship could eventually turn violent and abusive. These negative feelings will eventually kill any lingering positive elements within the relationship, to the extent that there is really no possibility in accepting the other party back and making a fresh start.

Fighting constantly is also another sure sign that something is wrong. When this happens, both parties will learn to go their own separate ways while still existing within the relationship. This of course is also very unhealthy as both parties will eventually develop such animosity towards each other, that they will eventually only exist bodily within the relationship, without any mental or physical contact. This will then no longer be a relationship at all.

Chapter 8- Always Find a Solution and Not Problem

Whether you have been married for only a brief period of time, many years, or even decades, you want your marriage to be the best that it can be! Not only do you and your spouse deserve happiness, this book will give you all of the helpful tips and advice to show you how to have exactly that!

You may have encountered some serious difficulties in your marriage, or you may simply wish to improve what is already a good relationship. The good news is you do not need to be content with wishing-- you can reconstruct your marriage, and start well on your way to building a lifelong love!

If you think about it, you may have noticed how often people try to find solutions to a problem without being sure what the problem actually is. You may also have noticed that attempting to resolve a problem in this manner is futile-- in fact, it is nearly impossible!

In order to find a solution, it is essential to make acknowledging the problem the very first step. While it would seem that this should "go without saying," you would be surprised at how many people miss it entirely, and try to rush headfirst into possible solutions without fully acknowledging what difficulties they are up against.

With this in mind, you can avoid the time-consuming, frustrating trap which too many fall into; and, instead, start at the beginning.

You can begin by asking yourself what problems you and your spouse are encountering. You will then know what difficulties need to be resolved, and what you wish to accomplish. A good way to go about this is to read through this book, and after you have thought about the topics contained within, get together with your spouse for a discussion. You can share your thoughts and feelings, and ask your spouse to share his or hers. Not only will this help in making progress toward finding solutions, it will also open up the lines of communication.

So, what kinds of problems are occurring in your marriage? Are you and your spouse losing touch with each other from basic lack of communication? Do you feel as if you are growing apart, and no longer feel as if you have an active place in each other's lives? Are there disagreements, or arguments, over such factors as money, jobs, children, and other people? Are you and your spouse considering a separation-- or, even worse, a divorce?

These, as well as most other factors which can cause a marital relationship to fall apart, can be resolved. You do not need a pile of "modern" books or other fads; and except in the most extreme cases, you do not need "couples counseling" or therapy. You can begin to put your marriage back together, reconstruct the joy that you both experienced at the beginning, and use both that initial joy and your mature experiences to make your marriage stronger and happier than ever!

After you have put some careful thought into acknowledging what problems you are confronting, it is also important to decide what you wish to accomplish. Do you want more quality time with your spouse? Do you want to be able to come to agreements, or respect for different stands, on various important issues?

One important point to keep in mind is that goals for a marriage are as individual as the people are individual. What this means is that what may be ideal for your friend or your sibling may not be so ideal for you and your spouse; unfortunately, it may also mean that what you want is not the same as what your spouse wants.

However, while the best time to have come to conclusions about the kind of marriage, goals and ideals that you both want was before you were married, even if you are just now encountering these differences it is never too late to resolve your differences and reach a common ground which you both should find acceptable.

Have you assessed the problem and discovered the specific difficulties which you are confronting? Have you put careful thought into deciding on the goals you wish to accomplish? Good for you! You have taken the first important steps! Your marriage is not only worth preserving and improving-- you can make it happier and stronger than ever!

Lines of Communication

In order for any relationship to be successful, there must be consistent good communication. Although this is true for any relationship, it is most essential in marriage. In nearly every marriage which has begun to deteriorate, lack of communication is one of the main factors.

One of the best ways to resolve this problem is to go back to the very beginning-- your beginning! Was lack of communication a problem all along, or is it a something which started at some particular point in time?

For many couples, lack of communication was a problem since the onset of their relationship. If you and your spouse fall into this category, it is essential that you come to terms with this problem so that you can work on resolving it. Some people have had this lack of communication because they felt that "love would conquer all," and therefore did not recognize the need to discuss important issues; others have begun a relationship and even entered into marriage feeling unable to voice their thoughts, feelings, preferences, beliefs, and merely gone along with their partners on everything.

For people in these categories, the time usually comes when they are no longer content to simply "go with the flow," and find that major differences and disagreements occur when they attempt to assert themselves. They may find that their spouse wishes to remain in charge; or they may find that they and their spouse disagree on significant issues.

In either case, opening the lines of communication is the first, essential step in asserting oneself and in beginning to reach agreements. You will find that there will be a number of instances in which you and your spouse must "agree to disagree."

For many other couples, however, communication was a present factor in the beginning, but somehow managed to deteriorate over time. Lack of time with each other due to family and work responsibilities often account for many of these instances. Sometimes, also, a person's priorities shift-- while the marital relationship was once a person's number-one focus, other factors in his or her life led the marriage to take second-place, somehow not seeming as important as it was at the beginning.

In these instances, reassessing priorities is the main key to reestablishing good communication. It is necessary to give your marriage the time and attention it needs and deserves-- and to give your spouse the time and attention which he or she needs and deserves.

There are other instances in which people simply lack good communication skills. If this appears to describe you or your spouse, take heart-- good communication skills can be learned. Even if you are nonassertive, or do not know how to communicate effectively, it is a skill which you can learn-- by practice and experience.

Whichever of these categories describes you and your spouse, recognizing the foundation of the problem is the first step in resolving it.

What is good communication? When you and your spouse can talk with each other about all important subjects and even subjects which have no serious implications at all; when you can freely share what you think, feel, believe, want, like and dislike; when you can state your stand on important issues and listen to your spouse's, with mutual respect even when there are matters of disagreement; you can have good, effective communication.

Good communication comes from practice, experience, respect and the time which you are willing to put into it!

Back to the Beginning!

As every problem had a beginning, so did everything of a positive nature! Unfortunately, when many people set themselves to the task of trying to "fix" a failing marriage, they neglect to look at the initial positives-- all of those wonderful assets which were there at the very beginning of their marriage, and even prior to their marriage!

This is a mistake, when you are honestly looking at the problems which have arisen in your marriage which you need to resolve, it is essential to also remind yourself and your spouse of all of the positive strengths, qualities, and characteristics which brought you together in the first place!

Whether you have been married for a year or twenty years, this factor is equally relevant to all who seriously wish to improve their marriage. The reason for this should be obvious, while working through and resolving your difficulties is necessary, placing some focus and emphasis on your relationship's initial strengths is the main factor which will help you to strengthen it now and for the future.

What brought you and your spouse together? What accounted for you and this person making the decision to spend the rest of your lives together? Whether you and your spouse were starry-eyed young people who married after knowing each other for a very brief period of time, or whether you had been in each other's lives for many years, let your memory take you back to your beginning.

What qualities or characteristics did you find the most appealing in your spouse? What kinds of goals, hopes, plans and dreams did you both shares? As each person is an individual, the answers to these questions will be equally individual-- and they are as relevant to reconstructing the strengths and the joys in your marriage as any questions and answers you can possibly ask yourself!

No matter how hopeless your situation may seem, taking this little trip down Memory Lane is one of the most important steps you can take in reconstructing your marriage. It is quite likely that you will find that the factors which influenced your decision to marry still do exist-- they just need to be noticed again and made fresh, all over again!

While you are thinking about these factors, you may also find yourself recalling many things which you and your spouse shared back then. You may have loved taking part in some kind of activity that you both enjoyed, for example, but somewhere along the line other priorities started to take precedence and you no longer had time for it.

When you are planning to reconstruct your marriage, another strength which you can build on is those shared interests. Whether you and your spouse liked to participate in a sport, attend rock concerts, have picnics in the park on Sunday afternoons, those activities which you both mutually enjoyed were bonding experiences-- and there is no reason why you cannot do them now!

The purpose in going back to your beginning is to assess both the strengths which contributed to your marriage and the interests which you had in common. In doing so, you will recall the passion which you both had for your relationship and for each other. And when you can recall your initial passions, you will then be in a position to reclaim them-- the favorite pastimes, the goals and dreams; they are all still there, waiting to be uncovered and appreciated again!

Chapter 9- The Power of Two

It does not matter how old you are, how long you have been married, or how full of a daily schedule you and your spouse may happen to have-- for a troubled marriage to be reborn, or for an adequate marriage to be improved, after good communication the second most important factor is Time!

In order to thrive, a relationship needs attention; and in order to thrive, so do both partners!

These days we often hear a lot about "quality time." In many cases, however, this comes to mean trying to squeeze as much as possible into a small amount of time allotted for it. People whose everyday lives and schedules are full to the overflowing point with job and family obligations usually consider this to be the only alternative; but there are also many whose personal interests, hobbies and pastimes take precedence, leaving the marital relationship to be resigned to this version of "quality time."

There are two problems associated with this concept. First, obviously, pre-scheduled quality time is simply not enough. However, the other significant factor in attempting to have a marital relationship without giving enough time to it is that when one spouse or both begins to see that neither the relationship nor he or she is a priority anymore, both the relationship and the spouse will suffer from the neglect.

If you think back to your early days with your spouse, you were in the majority if you and this person wished and attempted to spend every minute together. In a healthy, normal relationship, "I only have eyes for you" is indeed a truism-- there was nothing and no one that could compare with your new partner, nothing and no one that could pry your attention away from this person!

As is the case for normal, healthy couples, this begins to change. In most instances it is a matter of needing to work, tending to family responsibilities, and even having one's own particular interests and friends which causes the spouses to shift their focus off of each other and off of their relationship.

If you are preparing to reconstruct your marriage, rebuilding that initial relationship is necessary. One very important point which many in this situation miss, however, is that while being more generous with your time is essential, getting back to the way it was in placing more emphasis and focus on your partner is also essential. As the quickest way to cause a substantial feeling of neglect

Is to make that person feel as if he is not as important to you as he used to be, reemphasizing the fact that he is indeed a priority in your life will do wonders to bring the sense of connection and joy back into your marriage!

If you truly want your marriage to be the very best that it can be you cannot afford to be stingy with your time! Granting someone an hour per week, after all of the "more important" factors in your life have been taken care of, simply will not do it.

If you are like most people, you probably do not have the faintest clue in how to get more time for your spouse in your already-full schedule. The theory is correct: if you cannot find the time, you must make the time. We all know that finding free time is a luxury which most of us do not have; so if you look at it in those terms, you are not giving it a chance.

Instead, seeing your spouse and your relationship as a real priority in your life which you must make time for is the key. Perhaps you can look at it in a manner similar to the way in which you view your job: it is necessary, it is good, and the time will be taken for it.

If you have come to or past the point where spending a significant amount of time with your spouse is something which you have not done for a long period of time, it may feel like an unfamiliar venture. We all know people who have been married for many years, and rarely see each other because one or both individuals are "too busy." Perhaps this describes you-- or perhaps you see yourself heading in this direction, and are unsure as to what to do about it.

In addition to setting your spouse and your relationship as a priority again in matters of giving enough time, what you do with that time is also relevant. For example, you may know couples, such as retired older people, who spend a great deal of time together, yet do little together and have little to say to each other!

While being in each other's presence is generally a good thing in itself, simply "being there" can benefit from a little boost. While planning in advance for what you wish to do is not always a good idea, having something in mind can be quite helpful.

If you are as many people who have full schedules and little time, it is most beneficial if the time you put into your relationship is focused on your "togetherness." There is an aspect of this which many do not consider-- and that is that there are two very different manners in which couples spend their time together. One is a matter of focusing on each other; the second is a matter of putting more focus onto activities and/ or other people. And even though both are good, the former is much more helpful when the basic goal is to regain communication and togetherness.

If you are uncertain as to what this means, and what the difference is, you can think about it this way: if you and your spouse go out to dinner, a movie, a party, or participate in an activity, your general focus is on the activity. You are not giving your spouse the attention he or she may need, nor communicating effectively, when the focus is on enjoying a movie or interacting with other people at a party!

Having and sharing common interests, taking part in hobbies and pastimes, and socializing with other people is important to the individual as well as to the couple. However, viewing it as a significant part of "couple time" or "togetherness time" is a mistake, because it cannot fulfill that purpose. Instead, granting your spouse your undivided attention is the factor which will help this all-important person to realize that he or she still takes center-stage in your life!

Each person is an individual; and, as such, no two people can reasonably be expected to agree on everything. Being able to recognize this as a fact-of-life is one of the most important signs of maturity. It is also the first step in learning how to effectively resolve differences.

If you think about it, you probably know many people who do not have that level of maturity. Even though it affects every area of life, it can quickly spell "disaster" in a marriage! You may know someone who, due to flaws in his or her upbringing, always has to "have his own way." It may be someone who always had and did whatever he wanted as a child, and became older without growing up, still asserting his entitlement over "getting his way."

It may be someone who had to fight for everything that he had, and even as an adult sees any differences as a threat to "his rights." Or it may be someone who was spoiled, with "his way" never being challenged by anyone. While such a person can learn how to respectfully acknowledge differences, and learn how to compromise, it all depends on the willingness of that person.

Fortunately, difficulties in a marriage are not always to such an extreme. Perhaps you and your spouse did not fully acknowledge your differences in the early stages of your relationship; or perhaps you felt that time and love would solve the problem.

While effective communication is essential in resolving this type of problem, respect for each other's differences and the motivation to reach a solution are also necessary.

As differences come about primarily from a person's background and upbringing, there can be many or few, minor or serious. But whether the subject is a matter of a minor disagreement or something of a very serious nature, getting the hang of resolving differences before they become matters of confrontation is the most important factor.

In other words, what the issue is not nearly as relevant as what you do about it. Whether you and your spouse are disagreeing on something as tiny as where to hang your towels in your bathroom, or something of large proportion such as whether or not your sixteen-year-old is ready to get a driver's license, learning how to resolve differences is the deciding factor between reaching conclusions which both spouses can happily live with or allowing every difference to be a power-struggle of who wins and who loses. The fact of the matter is that in a marital relationship, if differences are settled by power-struggles, everyone loses.

If this has become a problem in your marriage, you may be wondering how it can work. There are two basic manners in which differences can be resolved-- by compromise, or by "agreeing to disagree."

In most cases, you will find that compromise is indeed the best solution. This way, a conclusion is reached which both persons can be relatively comfortable with. In some instances, however, agreeing to disagree is the only viable solution. The reason why it is most beneficial is that it eliminates power struggles and promotes respect between both people.

Although many people fail to grasp this fact, mainly due to their upbringing or popular trends, "fighting" is most definitely not an unavoidable, par-for-the-course part of any relationship, including marriage. The fact of the matter is that most arguments can be stopped in their tracks by setting yourself to the task of learning effective communication and how to resolve your differences through compromise and agreeing to disagree.

It is simply not necessary for any disagreement to escalate into a "fight"-- nor is it healthy! It causes more problems than were there to begin with, and diminishes the respect between the two individuals. Learning how to resolve differences is not only essential-- it is also possible!

The World is Not Just You

Regardless of how long you and your spouse have been married, you may have noticed that over time, more and more people have begun to populate your lives. On the other hand, it is possible that you have not even noticed it, or else have not yet realized that it can have a significant impact on your marriage.

While it is a fact of life that your marriage cannot be "an island unto itself," the influence of other people can often prove to be quite negative.

There are a number of ways in which this problem can occur. You or your spouse may have a family member who likes to meddle, or insists on being included in everything. You or your spouse may have a longtime close friend who displays those same characteristics. Your lives may also be populated by buddies-- the types of people with whom you enjoy various activities, in which your spouse may or may not participate. For many working couples, there is also the addition of co-workers and business associates.

In any normal, healthy adult's life, there are many people other than simply one's spouse. The problem with this can occur when one of the partners finds himself or herself in the position of "divided loyalties"-- who needs more time, who needs more attention, and which subjects and places should be "off limits" to everyone other than one's partner.

If one or both spouses have always been socially active, or extremely close with his or her family-of-origin, this can add to the difficulties. Spouses who have separate friends and separate interests can also encounter problems in knowing where to draw the line.

While it is unreasonable-- and unhealthy-- to expect two individuals to share all of the same associates, it can seriously damage the marital relationship if these other associates demand or receive significantly more time and attention than one's own spouse.

For example, even though spending every Sunday watching the ballgame on television with your buddies can be enjoyable recreation, it becomes intrusive and unfair to your spouse if your buddies take that afternoon pastime to mean that your food supply is up-for-grabs, or that they can simply stay and spend the night at your home whenever they wish to do so.

Similar difficulties can ensue if your parents or siblings feel that your home is theirs, without needing a phone call or an invitation, or if people with whom you associate in business expect your home to be little more than an extension of the workplace.

The problem of divided loyalties often reaches an extreme and places an unnecessary strain on a marriage when one spouse's friends are of the opposite sex. While many people have grown up with platonic friendships and do not see anything unusual about it, it can cause stress under any circumstances but most especially so when the other spouse did not have such arrangements in his or her own background.

In such instances, your spouse's concerns need to be addressed. While it is normal and important for each person to have friends, in the interest of both marital harmony and the well-being of both partners, it is nearly always unwise to pursue or persist in friendships which make the other spouse uncomfortable.

Whether the person or people in question are your family members, friends, or co-workers, the most important point to keep in mind is that your first loyalty is to the person you chose to marry!

Chapter 10- The Importance of Understanding Marriage Boundaries

One difficulty which arises in many marriages is the lack of boundaries. In some instances either or both spouses may not be clear about this subject; in other cases, other people in their lives can go a long way in creating the problem. It cannot be stressed too strongly: the very best, healthiest, happiest marriage is one where clear boundaries exist and are consistently respected by both spouses and those around them!

For some people, boundaries are a familiar way of life; for others, however, the concept is something which must be learned. A person's nuclear family and the environment of his or her upbringing makes up the manner in which the person views this subject; but it is no less relevant, regardless of one's background.

There are a number of boundaries which are essential for a healthy, happy marriage. One of the most important is the marital relationship itself. In a healthy marriage, both partners are aware of, and respect, the fact that certain things are between the two of them and should remain between the two of them.

Keeping each other's confidences is absolutely essential. The privacy between a husband and a wife is so universally-recognized that it is even protected by law! When your spouse shares with you something which is extremely private to him or her, he or she should be able to feel completely confident that you will not repeat this information to anyone. It does not matter whether you think the subject to be silly or frivolous, or a difficult burden which you may not wish to carry by yourself, or something which you think your friends may find "interesting"-- being able to keep private communications private is one of the main foundations of trust.

While we are on the subject of friends, it must also be said that you should resist sharing the problems of your marriage with your friends. Airing your grievances about your spouse, especially if done so on a regular basis, will not only undermine your marriage but can also serve to generate bad feelings between your friends and your partner. Even though everyone has a legitimate complaint every now and then, you should make a point of resisting the urge to fill your friends in on "What a jerk George is!" This habit does nothing but cause strife for everyone involved.

It is unfortunate to hear how many married couples believe that their sex life is also something which should be "up for discussion" with other people. The sexual relationship between a husband and wife should never be brought into the public view-- to do so destroys the intimacy which is one of the main parts of married life. Unless there is a serious difficulty which necessitates the assistance or intervention of a medical professional, a married couple's sexual relationship should never go any further than between the two of them.

Important boundaries are also violated when a spouse feels the need to solicit other people's opinions and input on subjects which should remain between the couple themselves. Although it is natural to want to know what others think about various issues, if there are matters of disagreement between you and your spouse it is unfair to attempt to get others on your side.

Some couples also experience problems with boundaries when one or the other person does not realize or does not respect the partner's individual boundaries. Even though it may seem odd in this modern day, there are still far too many married people who fully believe that their partners have no reason or right to personal privacy, personal space, or personal possessions.

In such cases it should be clearly and firmly stressed that simply because one has gotten married this does not mean he or she has ceased to be an individual person, or has ceased to have the right and the need for personal boundaries. Whether the problem has arisen due to one spouse's lack of full trust in the other person, or does not acknowledge the other person as a separate individual, or has the distasteful and destructive characteristics of needing power and control, it is a problem which must be resolved-- not only in the interest of the marriage, but also the well-being of both spouses. Such a person must learn that there is a difference between "Yours," "Mine," and "Ours"!

When other people do not acknowledge or do not respect your boundaries, this too can create huge problems if it is not addressed and resolved as quickly as possible. For example, you may have a meddlesome relative who consistently pries for information about your personal life, or a friend who believes that your home should be accessible to him or her at any hour of the day or night. In such instances, the best manner in which to deal with the situation is for you and your spouse to present a "united front" so that the intrusions are ended.

You may be familiar with the old saying about "building a hedge" around your marriage. Far from being an outdated concept, it not only continues to be true but continues to be the most important thing you can do to ensure a healthy, happy marriage.

In addition to the topics you just read about, which are universal to all married couples, individual needs also play a role. For example, you or your spouse may be uncomfortable with physical contact from the opposite sex, and feel that hugs should be reserved only for each other; or you may object to the other person's friends having an "open-door policy" on your refrigerator. These, and any number of other topics, are often very important to one spouse yet seem trivial to the other.

The point in resolving such potential conflicts before they become real problems is to reach a conclusion which both spouses can comfortably accept. The key is in taking your partner's needs and feelings into consideration-- and that should be your main priority. For you to place a boundary which is necessary for your spouse's well-being and peace of mind should not be seen as a sacrifice, but rather as a positive act.

Power-Struggle

One might be tempted to think that power-struggles are a thing of the past-- but anyone who has ever been in a relationship where one is present is fully aware that this concept is as valid, as troublesome, and as potentially destructive in this modern day as it ever was!

Power-struggles go way beyond one person wanting to be the deciding factor in topics of disagreement-- a true power-struggle exists when one partner insists on "running the show." In the worst of extremes, as often does happen, the result is that there is really no "marriage" at all, and the other partner begins to lose more and more of his or her personal selfhood.

If you are one of the lucky ones who has not experienced this, or if you have and need to understand it better in order to begin resolving it in your own marriage, it is difficult but it is not impossible.

Power-struggles usually begin from one person's ingrained beliefs about what is "right." One example is the notion that a man must have "authority" over his wife and his home; on the opposite side of the same coin is the idea that a "modern woman" is one-hundred-percent on her own, with little "use" for her husband at all. Needless to say, these are not very positive beliefs on which to build a marriage! It does need to be said, however-- because far too many people have already entered into a marriage with these types of concepts, and find that happiness and harmony will not occur.

When these extremes of power-struggles exist, unless they are resolved there can be only two possible results-- either the marriage will fail, or one spouse will fall apart. If both spouses have the willingness and motivation to resolve the problem, as well as the intelligence and personality traits needed to make doing so possible, it can often be resolved. In many cases, however, counseling is necessary-- because it is very difficult to shake destructive beliefs from a person when he has held them for much of his life.

The Sail of Marriage
There are generally two forms of power-struggles. One is the type where one person insists on "running things," and the other is the type where one person shuts the spouse out of his or her life. The ability to resolve this problem rests in both spouses' willingness and readiness to acknowledge two main points: first, that a true marriage "takes two," and, as such, each person's beliefs, needs, feelings, and input are equally essential; and second, that each is an individual person who cannot be taken advantage of, silenced, or dismissed.

Whether you have been married for a short period of time or many decades, a common factor in this problem is that many fail to recognize when a power-struggle becomes actual abuse. Although this word has become a popular "catch-phrase," used far too lightly and when it does not apply, it often exists without a person being fully aware of it.

A power-struggle does not have to result in physical, sexual, or even verbal violence in order to be "abuse." This fact is the reason why many-- usually, but not always, women-- are in the position of being abused for years and even decades. They believe, erroneously, that if the person has not hit them, they are not being abused.

However, even if a power-struggle never escalates to physical violence, other forms of abuse which often occur are equally devastating, and equally destructive. If this sounds odd, the fact is that if a person is abused for a period of time, it has a damaging effect on her mind, her emotions, and her self-esteem.

It is abuse if your spouse exerts control over you, your actions, your life; this can range from telling you what you can and cannot wear, with whom you can and cannot associate, or where you can and cannot go. It is abusive if he monitors your actions, your whereabouts, and your privacy. It is abusive if your feelings, thoughts, beliefs and needs are dismissed as irrelevant or inconsequential. It is abusive if you are frequently put-down, ridiculed, accused or threatened. It is abusive if you are made to feel that you are accountable to your spouse, or if you are made to feel weak, small, helpless, afraid, unintelligent, unattractive, or unworthy.

While these actions are the foundation of an extreme power-struggle, they are also abuse. It is not something which you should tolerate; it is not something which you should ask advice from your friends about; it is a life-diminishing situation for which you need professional assistance.

Depending on the magnitude of the situation, its duration, the personality of your spouse, and the effects which it is having on you, this can mean professional counseling, legal intervention, or both. Do not make the mistake of believing or hoping that it well get better on its own, or that your spouse will "change"-- if you are being abused, reach out for help!

Happiness

Of course it sounds like a ridiculous question! How could anyone possibly not know what the word 'happiness' means?! The fact of the matter, though, is that many people have never really thought about it-- and, if you are reading this book, you and your spouse may not even know if you both have the same definitions!

As an individual, and as a married couple, you want happiness! As an individual, and as a married couple, you deserve it! Fortunately, it is one of those elusive subjects which, with a little careful thought and consideration, can become very clear-- and when what happiness means to you is clear to you, you will then be in the best position to claim this wonderful, life-affirming quality for yourselves!

If you and your spouse are like most average American adults, when the question is posed to you "What does the word 'happiness' mean to you?" you will probably not have a quick answer. Perhaps you have never put much thought into it, assuming that happiness is something which is either "there" or not. The only problem with this is that in order to attain and maintain happiness, you must first have some ideas as to what it means to you.

There are a number of ways to look at this subject. Some people define happiness in terms of something external, others in terms of the internal, and still others in terms of acceptance.

It is not as complicated as it may sound! The key is in realizing your own personal definition, and, in order to greatly enhance your marriage, "compare notes" with your spouse!

Those who view happiness in external terms are generally those who are the most driven. These folks see happiness as being the result of what they do, have, and accomplish. This type of person is happy, for example, when he has earned a great job promotion through hard work, has purchased a brand-new car, or is taking the family on a two-week vacation. His ability to be happy is directly influenced and affected by what is around him.

The person who finds happiness from an internal source is usually the type of person who is calm, rational, and content. He is the person who cares more about who he is rather than what he has or does, and sees other people in the same manner.

The people who define happiness in terms of acceptance are sometimes mislabeled as settled, unmotivated, or boring. While this kind of person is fully capable of dealing with whatever comes his way, and is as effective at doing so as anyone else, his general outlook involves not wishing to make waves, taking things as they are, and not liking any type of radical change unless it is necessary.

While these three types of people are different from each other and approach life much differently, it is nothing more than basic personality-traits. The good news is that even those who are married to someone who possesses a different style can have a happy, harmonious marriage. All it really takes is understanding your own personal "happiness style" and being aware of and respecting your spouse's! With that in mind, happiness can be yours-- for a lifetime!

CHAPTER 11- THOSE YEARS TOGETHER

It does not matter whether you have been married for one year or thirty years; it does not matter what kinds of career or family responsibilities you may have, or the state of your health, or how much money you have. What does matter is that in addition to saving your marriage, your wish is to make it the very best, the very happiest-- and doing so means stepping aside for a moment, stepping aside from your average, daily life, and reconstructing those all-important factors which gave your marriage its initial vision.

Take just a moment to look back throughout the duration of your marriage. How much of its original strength, vibrancy, and all-out enthusiasm gave way to general day-to-day life with its obligations, worries, and routines?

Instead of focusing too much energy on how much has been lost, take heart in the fact that much of it can be regained.

If you are like most adults, you are probably thinking this is foolish. After all, you are not as young as you used to be; and after all, there are also many time-consuming factors in your everyday life which you did not have in the past!

Some of us, however, have duly noted that one amazing benefit to growing a little older is the ability to stand in the present-day while looking both backward and forward-- at the way things were and at the way we would like for them to become.

Regardless of your current age or situation, you can have this benefit, also! You can begin by looking back at the early days of your marriage, and invest a bit of time in recalling what was important to you and your spouse. I'm not referring to how ideal your everyday life was at that time; but instead, the visions which you both had-- your dreams, your goals.

If you were like most couples, those dreams and goals probably included you both together. Perhaps you were both socially-aware, and dreamed of someday joining the Peace Corps together and helping those who were less fortunate. Perhaps you had an idea of beginning some type of a business of your own. Whatever your particular dreams were, they somehow took second-place and then eventually vanished when you and your spouse began to take on the basic responsibilities of adult life.

Now is the time to assess your dreams-- and when you do, you may be pleasantly surprised to find that the idealistic dreams you had in the past are still an option for you. These days, we are all much more fortunate than generations past-- for even growing older does not impose the limitations as it once did. In fact, there are more and more opportunities opening up for older people than ever before-- careers, travel, and numerous other options.

The Sail of Marriage

You and your spouse may decide that the dreams of your youth are no longer relevant or are unreasonable, for one reason or another. If this is the case, you can decide on new dreams together-- and begin putting them into motion. Perhaps it is something you can do ten years into the future, or perhaps it is something that you can do now!

What is the purpose of dreaming, and of making plans to put those dreams into action? One important factor is that everyone needs something to look forward to; but the other, equally-essential factor, is that it will go a long way in re-creating the bond that you and your spouse once had.

Having a dream is great-- but sharing a dream together is even better! And when you are in the process of turning those dreams into reality, you will see that the love and connection of your early marriage is not only still clearly present, but stronger than ever before!

Helpful Tips

If you have read this far, you should be well on your way to improving your marriage-- not only resolving the difficulties which led you to read this book in the first place, but also to make your marriage stronger, healthier, and happier than you had ever expected it could be.

Instead of summarizing a book which you have already read, perhaps you will find some additional tips to be helpful! Depending on your own experience, you may or may not already know how often seemingly-small things can add up to huge problems or confrontations; and this is especially true for overworked, over-tired adults who can occasionally or frequently say or do something without realizing that it may have an impact.

When you are in the process of reconstructing your marriage and your relationship with your spouse, one important point to keep in mind is that while spontaneity in action can create enjoyable results, being too spontaneous with speech often does not! While this does not mean having to carefully guard everything that you say, it is most beneficial to your newfound communication if you develop the habit of thinking before you speak. Too often it happens that a person at the end of a long, exhausting day will blurt out something hurtful, or something which will be misinterpreted. Be careful with your words-- for they have great impact, for better or for worse!

You may be familiar with the old saying that honesty is the best policy. In the interest of your marriage and your relationship, it is a good idea to balance that saying with "be kind." Whether the subject is something which you yourself would consider trivial, such as your wife appearing ten pounds heavier in her new outfit, or whether you have made the mistake of being drawn into the popular "honesty kick" where nothing whatsoever should be kept private, balance your truthfulness with the knowledge of how what you wish to say will impact your spouse's feelings.

If your marriage is your priority, do your best to eliminate distractions. In an average couple's life, there are already more than enough distractions in everyday life; it is neither necessary nor recommended to emphasize the past over the present-day. Unless there is something which could truly have an impact on your marriage or your life, leave your past in the past.

While adult life does contain some degree of negativity, you will be promoting the health and happiness of your marriage, as well as both your spouse and yourself, if you develop the habit of focusing on the positives. In other words, if there is something which needs to be dealt with or addressed, by all means do it-- but resist the impulse to make complaining a part of your everyday life.

When you have come to terms with the differences between Yours, Mine, and Ours, it is essential to grant enough time to each. Constant togetherness is not only unhealthy, it is a direct opposition to many people's personalities. While you should be sure to make plenty of time for togetherness, it is just as important to grant personal time and space to both your spouse and yourself.

If you feel the need for professional advice or intervention, by all means seek the help that you need. If, however, your marriage simply needs a little closer examination, resolving of basic difficulties, and better communication, all it takes is the willingness and motivation on your part and your spouse's part to gain all of this valuable insight and turn your marriage into a lifelong love!

ABOUT THE AUTHOR

Juliet Williams is a down to earth type of person. She always takes every achievement with humility and every challenge. When she married to John she has to admit that her life was never easy. You have to deal every challenge together or else marriage will break.

Juliet understands that there are a lot of broken marriages and some, no longer believe in marriage. That's they time that she decided to help married couple stay together and become a marriage counselor. Juliet lives in Long Island with her family.

www.ingramcontent.com/pod-product-compliance
Lightning Source LLC
Chambersburg PA
CBHW070042260726
48658CB00002B/693